Challenging
WORD
GAMES

Mayme Allen &
Janine Kelsch

W9-CKB-460

Sterling Publishing Co., Inc.
New York

Illustrations by Mayme Allen

Edited by Laurel Ornitz

Our special thanks to Chris Powell and David Hruska for
their supportive assistance

3   5   7   9   10   8   6   4

Published by Sterling Publishing Company, Inc.
387 Park Avenue South, New York, N.Y. 10016
A slightly different version was previously
published under the title *101 Word Puzzlers*
© 1997 by Mayme Allen & Janine Kelsch
Distributed in Canada by Sterling Publishing
% Canadian Manda Group, One Atlantic Avenue, Suite 105
Toronto, Ontario, Canada M6K 3E7
Distributed in Great Britain and Europe by Cassell PLC
Wellington House, 125 Strand, London WC2R 0BB, England
Distributed in Australia by Capricorn Link (Australia) Pty Ltd.
P.O. Box 6651, Baulkham Hills, Business Centre, NSW 2153, Australia
Manufactured in the United States of America
All rights reserved

Sterling ISBN 0-8069-9854-7

For our parents,
Pete and Cindy McDaniel
and
John and Georgia Kelsch

CONTENTS

CIRCLE SEARCH

General Instructions

In each of the following puzzles, all of the words listed can be found in the letter grid they accompany. Answers appear vertically, horizontally, diagonally, and backwards, but remember—*circle only the letters of each word*, and not the word itself. When you've finished, the letters left uncircled spell a secret answer not included in the list!

CIRCLE SEARCH #1

All in a Day's Work

Amateur Golfer
Artist
Bartender
Biker
Brigand
Caretaker
Commander
Cop
Dancer
Engineer

Entomologist
Farrier
Flight
   Attendant
Florist
Hobo
Intern
Majorette
Manager
Marine

Metallurgist
Movie Star
Musician
Navigator
Notary
Nun
Nurse
Osteopath
Plasterer
Poet

Porter
Race Driver
Retailer
Stylist
Teacher
Vet
Yeoman

```
R  E  C  N  A  D  S  M  U  S  I  C  I  A  N

E  N  B  A  R  T  E  N  D  E  R  O  U  U  A

I  T  R  E  T  A  I  L  E  R  R  M  N  G  V

R  O  E  B  I  K  E  R  Y  E  O  M  A  N  I

R  M  E  R  S  R  E  R  E  T  S  A  L  P  G

A  O  N  I  T  R  A  N  R  E  T  N  I  E  A

F  L  I  G  H  T  A  T  T  E  N  D  A  N  T

L  O  G  A  O  O  H  T  A (P)(O)(E)(T) S  O

O  G  N  N  B  N  E  C  S  P  O  R  T  E  R

R  I  E  D  O  R  H  G  E  E  S  R  U  N  E

I  S  N  E  O  E  S  T  Y  L  I  S  T  I  G

S  T  R  J  R  A  C  E  D  R  I  V  E  R  A

T  C  A  R  E  T  A  K  E  R  A  E  O  A  N

L  M  R  E  F  L  O  G  R  U  E  T  A  M  A

C  O  P  T  S  I  G  R  U  L  L  A  T  E  M
```

CIRCLE SEARCH #2

Shopping for Values

Accordance	Fidelity	Kindness	Spirit
Amity	Forbearance	Love	Sympathy
Bravery	Forgiveness	Mercy	Temperance
Candor	Generosity	Patience	Tolerance
Charity	Harmony	Piety	Truth
Courage	Honor	Pity	Valor
Empathy	Hope	Prudence	
Fairness	Humility	Purity	
Faith	Justness	Righteousness	

```
P  R  U  D  E  N  C  E  C  N  E  I  T  A  P

S  P  R  O  N  O  H  U  M  I  L  I  T  Y  H

S  T  O  L  E  R  A  N  C  E  I  E  L  E  P

E  Y  A  C  C  O  R  D  A  N  C  E  F  C  U

N  T  M  T  I  R  I  P  S  N  M  O  H  N  R

D  I (L) P  I  E  T  Y  A  P  R  T  S  A  I

N  S (O) A  A  R  Y  R  A  G  I  S  N  R  T

I  O (V) T  U  T  E  T  I  A  E  H  R  A  Y

K  R (E) T  I  P  H  V  F  N  H  O  P  E  E

C  E  H  M  M  Y  E  Y  R  E  V  A  R  B  G

A  N  A  E  C  N  O  I  R  O  L  A  V  R  A

N  E  T  R  E  H  A  R  M  O  N  Y  P  O  R

D  G  E  S  I  F  Y  T  I  L  E  D  I  F  U

O  M  S  S  E  N  T  S  U  J  P  I  T  Y  O

R  I  G  H  T  E  O  U  S  N  E  S  S  C  C
```

CIRCLE SEARCH #3
Fowl Play

Albatross
Anhinga
Ani
Auk
Avocet
Bufflehead
Canvasback
Caracara
Chat
Cormorant
Crane

Cuckoo
Dowitcher
Duck
Eagle
Grackle
Grebe
Gull
Heron
Ibis
Kingfisher
Meadowlark

Moa
Muscovy
Oriole
Owl
Pheasant
Phoebe
Prairie
   Chicken
Ptarmigan
Rail
Rhea

Ruff
Smew
Sora
Stilt
Tanager
Titmouse
Woodpecker
Wren

```
E  A  G  L  E  R  E  H  S  I  F  G  N  I  K
B  U  F  F  L  E  H  E  A  D  E  N  A  R  C
E  K  M  L  F  E  O  R  G  O  L  I  A  R  A
R  B  U  A  R  U  E  U  R  W  T  Y  R  E  B
G  G  E  O  N  G  R  I  A  I  E  V  A  K  S
M  N  N  O  A  I  O  I  C  T  C  O  R  C  A
N  O  R  N  H  L  N  E  K  C  O  C  A  E  V
A  G  A  H  E  P  S  T  L  H  V  S  C  P  N
G  T  D  R  E  U  N  O  E  E  A  U  A  D  A
I  B  I  S  O  A  T  N  A  R  O  M  R  O  C
M  W  E  M  S  S  A  N  H  I  N  G  A  O  U
R  V  T  A  L  B  A  T  R  O  S  S  C  W  C
A  I  E  W  E  M  E  A  D  O  W  L  A  R  K
T  H  O  K  C  U  D  H  T  L  I  T  S  E  O
P  R  A  I  R  I  E  C  H  I  C  K  E  N  O
```

8

CIRCLE SEARCH #4

Up a Tree

Apple	Coconut Palm	Maple	Plum
Ash	Date Palm	Mesquite	Poplar
Balsa	Ebony	Mimosa	Quince
Banyan	Elderberry	Monkeypod	Redwood
Baobab	Elm	Mulberry	Sycamore
Bean	Fir	Oak	Teak
Beech	Ginkgo	Olive	Tree of Heaven
Birch	Grapefruit	Orange	Walnut
Chestnut	Gum	Pear	Yew
Chinaberry	Juniper	Pecan	
Clove	Lime	Pine	

```
D  O  P  Y  E  K  N  O  M  I  M  O  S  A  E
A  G  I  N  K  G  O  T  L  N  A  C  E  P  R
T  R  E  E  O  F  H  E  A  V  E  N  K  A  O
E  A (P)(L)(U)(M) C  M  P  M  A  P  L  E  M
P  P  H  D  E  U  R  I  T  U  N  L  A  W  A
A  E  J  E  R  G  I  L  U  E  N  I  P  S  C
L  F  Y  R  R  E  B  A  N  I  H  C  L  O  Y
M  R  C  B  A  M  D  S  O  H  K  A  E  T  S
U  U  H  E  P  L  L  W  C  E  B  O  N  Y  B
L  I  E  R  P  E  P  E  O  R  A  N  G  E  N
B  T  S  R  L  C  E  O  C  O  A  U  E  V  A
E  H  T  Y  E  N  A  A  P  E  D  C  V  O  Y
R  S  N  E  F  I  R  T  B  R  H  E  I  L  N
R  A  U  W  J  U  N  I  P  E  R  E  L  C  A
Y  E  T  I  U  Q  S  E  M  B  A  B  O  A  B
```

CIRCLE SEARCH #5
Globe Trotting

Africa
Afghanistan
Algeria
Argentina
Australia
Austria
Bolivia
Chile
China

Cuba
El Salvador
Finland
Germany
Great Britain
Greece
Iceland
Iran
Ireland

Italy
Korea
Laos
Mali
New Guinea
Nigeria
Nova Scotia
Pakistan
Poland

Soviet Union
Sri Lanka
Sweden
United States
Venezuela
Wales

```
A C I R F A N I T N E G R A W
U C H R C Z D N A L N I F A N
S N H I A I R E G I N G L D I
T E I I N N E R S O H E R N A
R W D T L A E W I A S R O A T
I G N C E E E N N N H M D L I
A U A O C D U I O N B A A E R
I I L E E T S V A O S N V C B
L N O N E T A T L O A Y L I T
A E P I A S S I A S L L A K A
R A V N C I V L O T G V S O E
T O A O K I T A L Y E K L R R
S I T A A K N A L I R S E E G
U I P D N A L E R I I (I)(L)(A)(M)
A L E U Z E N E V A A A B U C
```

CIRCLE SEARCH #6
Catch of the Day

Barracuda
Bass
Blenny
Bonito
Carp
Chub
Clown Fish
Cod
Coney
Coral

Crappie
Damselfish
Drum
Eel
Gar
Marlin
Octopus
Oyster
Peacock
Flounder

Perch
Pike
Puffer Fish
Red Snapper
Roe
Ruff
Sardine
Scorpion Fish
Shad
Sharknose Goby

Shrimp
Spotted
Dolphin
Squid
Starfish
Sting Ray
Tarpon
Tuna
Wrasse

```
H  N  I  H  P  L  O  D  D  E  T  T  O  P  S
S  H  A  R  K  N  O  S  E  G  O  B  Y  P  Q
I  S  G  Y  G  B  R  C  H  U  B  E  M  E  U
F  I  B  A  E  B  A  S  S  D  E  I  A  K  I
N  F  O  N  R  N  I  R  A  L  R  E  R  I  D
O  R  N  U  A  F  O  M  R  H  T  W  L  P  R
I  A  I  T  N  C  S  C  S  A  R  D  I  N  E
P  T  T  W  T  E  L  I  T  E  C  H  N  O  P
R  S  O  O  L  A  F  B  I  P  I  U  T  P  P
O  L  P  F  R  R  L  P  N  R  E  E  D  R  A
C  U  I  O  E  E  P  S  G  A  H  R  U  A  N
S  S  C  F  N  A  T  A  R  C  U  F  C  T  S
H  O  F  N  R  O  E  S  A  M  F  R  K  H  D
D  U  Y  C (D)(A)(H)(S) Y  W  R  A  S  S  E
P  E  A  C  O  C  K  F  L  O  U  N  D  E  R
```

CIRCLE SEARCH #7

In Your Element

Aluminum	Lead	Platinum	Thallium
Americium	Magnesium	Plutonium	Thorium
Antimony	Mendelevium	Promethium	Tin
Argon	Mercury	Radium	Titanium
Boron	Neon	Radon	Uranium
Calcium	Nickel	Silicon	Xenon
Carbon	Nitrogen	Sodium	Yttrium
Helium	Oxygen	Sulfur	Zinc
Iron	Phosphorus	Tantalum	Zirconium

```
T  H  A  L  L  I  U  M  U  I  N  A  T  I  T
A  L  E  K  C  I  N  R  U  F  L  U  S (N) H
N  N  E  G  Y  X  O  O  S  I  L  U (I) M  O
T  M  M  M  D  C  C  V  R  E  R (T) R  U  R
A  P  U  U  A  N  I  T  R  O  G  E  N  I  I
L  L  I  I  E  I  L  A  H  M  B  M  M  V  U
U  U  S  C  L  Z  I  P  U  U  N  U  N  E  M
M  T  E  L  D  E  S  I  G  I  I  I  O  L  U
U  O  N  A  O  O  H  M  X  N  R  D  G  E  I
N  N  G  C  H  T  U  E  A  O  O  O  R  D  C
I  I  A  P  E  I  N  R  L  C  N  S  A  N  I
T  U  M  M  D  O  U  C  A  R  B  O  N  E  R
A  M  O  A  N  A  L  U  M  I  N  U  M  M  E
L  R  R  N  O  D  A  R  D  Z  N  O  E  N  M
P  M  U  I  R  T  T  Y  N  O  M  I  T  N  A
```

TRIPLE PLAY

General Instructions

Each of the games that follow lists three definitions. The letters in the answers to the first and second definitions form the answer to the third definition when you rearrange the letters. See the following example.

EXAMPLE

Globe; sphere   *orb*
A bird's crop   *craw*
Lever-like tool   *crowbar*

TRIPLE PLAY #1

1. Easily reached
   Equipment for particular task
   Shrub with large, showy
      flowers

2. Potbelly
   Spool for winding line
   Elf who can reveal hidden
      treasure

3. Animals hunted for sport
      or food
   Narrow channel connecting
      bodies of water
   Civil officer empowered to
      enforce law

4. Large brass wind instrument
   Sticky, slippery substance
   To redirect energy of impulse

5. To draw liquid from
   Ice-cream holder
   Statute enacted by government

6. Insect
   Excessive desire
   To envy the possession of

7. Area where actors perform
   Mentally deficient person
   Person who enjoys good food

8. To bring into contact
   Play division
   Shield-shaped surface for
      family crest

9. Color; inexperienced
   Pillared structure over water
   Large, swift falcon

14

10. Sand ridge caused by wind _____
    Used in rowing _____
    Short, lyrical poem _____

TRIPLE PLAY #2

1. Thick, sticky black liquid _____
   Fanatical person _____
   Ship's quarantine station _____

2. Tracts of heather-covered
   open land _____
   Metal drawn into long thread _____
   Causing worry or anxiety _____

3. Small portion of something
   to drink _____
   2,000 pounds _____
   Caustic; sarcastic _____

4. Cud-chewing animal _____
   Organism that can cause
   disease _____
   Pledging of property to creditor _____

5. To defraud; to swindle _____
   Total of two figures _____
   Hair on man's upper lip _____

6. Small piece of rock _____
   To walk with lame leg _____
   Person easily deceived; fool _____

7. Hearing organ _____
   Channel through which liquid
   moves _____
   To defame; to slander _____

8. Contest or match _____
   Class of troops trained for sea _____
   Shallow hand drum with metal
   disks _____

9. Person's lot or fortune   _____
   Center of activity, attention _____
   To smother; to suppress   _____

10. To appear to be   _____
    Food (slang)   _____
    To immerse in liquid   _____

TRIPLE PLAY #3

1. Brace in bicycle wheel   _____
   Pleasant; agreeable   _____
   Receiving tube used in
      television   _____

2. Very sensitive or perceptive _____
   Five-petalled fragrant flower _____
   Thin oil distilled from
      petroleum   _____

3. Total of two numbers   _____
   Larger of two bones in forearm _____
   College graduate   _____

4. Night-flying insect   _____
   Brief, light sleep   _____
   Apparition; specter   _____

5. Proof of authenticity on
      document   _____
   Highest surface of anything _____
   Any of the twelve disciples _____

6. Device that broadcasts music _____
   Public promenade   _____
   Mammal with armorlike
      covering   _____

7. To provide food to group   ———————————
   Intense; profound   ———————————
   To feel and express
      disapproval of   ———————————

8. Mental condition based on such
      factors as sense of purpose
      and confidence in future   ———————————
   Compelling; convincing   ———————————
   Corporation formed by merger   ———————————

9. To end; to quash   ———————————
   Actor's part in play   ———————————
   To state in great detail; to give
      added information   ———————————

10. Small, hard seed   ———————————
    White-liquid drink   ———————————
    Old female cat   ———————————

TRIPLE PLAY #4

1. To injure by exertion   ———————————
   Playing card with one spot   ———————————
   To find out with certainty   ———————————

2. Piece of furniture used
      in dining   ———————————
   Strong wind; outburst   ———————————
   Something of little value   ———————————

3. Classification given to nouns in
      certain languages   ———————————
   Immoral habit   ———————————
   Difference; variation from
      the norm   ———————————

4. Grey matter   ———————————
   Container made of metal   ———————————
   Brilliant red; vermillion   ———————————

5. Fixed ratio; proportion
   Alcoholic liquor
   Error in printing or writing

   _____
   _____
   _____

6. Hockey players score points
      with this
   To bend the head forward
   Long, narrow canal boat

   _____
   _____
   _____

7. To condescend
   To rip; to rend
   To disparage one's character;
      to defame

   _____
   _____

   _____

8. Flexible series of joined links
   To wander; to rove
   Small mouth instrument

   _____
   _____
   _____

9. Bird's home
   System of meshed, toothed
      wheels
   To turn away; to alienate

   _____

   _____
   _____

10. Highest point of anything
    Coal scuttle
    Invertebrate animal with
       six feet

    _____
    _____

    _____

TRIPLE PLAY #5

1. Wet, sticky earth
   Relatively close
   Hard wood at center of
      tree trunk

   _____
   _____

   _____

2. Partly decayed plant matter
   Action without thought
   Short, amusing musical play

   _____
   _____
   _____

3. Sharp projecting point
   Penny, nickel, or dime
   Tobacco's poisonous ingredient

   _____
   _____
   _____

18

4. Sponsorship; auspices   _____
   Member of laboring class   _____
   Act or practice of spying   _____

5. Used in solution to stiffen
       fabrics   _____
   Fish eggs   _____
   Large group of musicians   _____

6. Belly button   _____
   Communist (slang)   _____
   Pale shade of purple   _____

7. Great affection and desire   _____
   To express deep sorrow   _____
   Wishing evil or harm to others   _____

8. Conceited; proud   _____
   Past tense of run   _____
   State of perfect blessedness   _____

9. Vessel used to transport water   _____
   Satellite of the earth   _____
   Pale-yellow horse   _____

10. Line of connected railroad cars   _____
    Association of people for some
        common objective   _____
    Substance for reducing friction   _____

TRIPLE PLAY #6

1. Tense and abrupt   _____
   Not any   _____
   In art, painting of a night scene   _____

2. To be prolific; to abound   _____
   Smell; stench   _____
   Car's instrument for measuring
       mileage   _____

3. Wingless parasitic insect
   Small roll
   Unclear; indefinite; vague
   _____
   _____
   _____

4. Money deposited with court
   Strong fibre used for
     making rope
   To rejoice; to exalt
   _____
   _____
   _____

5. To converse; to talk (slang)
   Adhesive strip
   Wall protecting troops from
     enemy fire
   _____
   _____
   _____

6. Manner of walking
   Anything that tempts, entices
   Tying or binding together
   _____
   _____
   _____

7. Old-fashioned pen
   Term of endearment
   Square dance using four
     couples
   _____
   _____
   _____

8. Landed estate
   Fixed bench in church
   Collective strength of
     the people
   _____
   _____
   _____

9. Small droplets of moisture
   Furious, uncontrolled anger
   Source of hay fever; common
     pollen
   _____
   _____
   _____

10. To grumble; to gripe
    Long-tailed rodent
    Substitute; in place of
    _____
    _____
    _____

TRIPLE PLAY #7

1. Withered old woman
   To search carefully for
   Short, thick staff; policeman's
      baton
   _____

2. Product of crying
   Moveable structure in entrance
   Bullfighter
   _____

3. Illusions produced by sleight
      of hand
   Monetary unit of Rumania
   Thick, sticky adhesive
      substance
   _____

4. Layer of paint; jacket
   To require
   Short, entertaining story
   _____

5. To gather a harvest
   Hardwood used for carving
   Small, slender parrot with
      long tail
   _____

6. Greedy, stingy person
   Country person; rustic
   To pay back to someone
   _____

7. Yellowish part of milk
   Oriental sauce
   Shade tree of Egypt
   _____

8. Woman ruler of monarchy
   Voucher for small sum
   Method of procedure
   _____

9. Transitional period
   Additional amount
   System of signalling
   _____

10. To be an omen of; to portend _____
Naïve _____
Genuine; in good faith _____

TRIPLE PLAY #8

1. To pull by forcible twisting
movement _____
Land measure _____
Perennial plant used primarily
in salads _____

2. To exhaust emotionally or
physically _____
Adult male _____
High-ranking public official of
China _____

3. Late-afternoon reception _____
Rich part of milk _____
To soften by steeping or
soaking _____

4. Opening for passage in wall
or fence _____
Pear-shaped stringed musical
instrument _____
Instruction of an individual _____

5. Contest; match _____
Reddish-brown color _____
Violent expression of feeling _____

6. Tactic intended to frustrate
opponent _____
Downy surface on cloth _____
Full suit of armor _____

7. Quality or conduct deserving
   reward   _____
   To look intently or curiously   _____
   Outer boundary of area   _____

8. Disk for tuning in channels   _____
   Lion's greeting   _____
   To convict quickly with
   questionable evidence   _____

9. To long intensely for something   _____
   Mentally quick; clever   _____
   Herb grown for flavoring and
   aroma   _____

10. To utter taunting words   _____
    Crustacean with short, broad
    shell   _____
    Card game using board
    and pegs   _____

REEL CHALLENGE

General Instructions

The following puzzles will test your knowledge of the silver screen. All are "triple features," with each movie connected by a common word to the one that follows or precedes it. For example:

Pillow _____ _____ Days

would become

Pillow <u>Talk</u> <u>Radio</u> Days
(Pillow Talk, Talk Radio, Radio Days)

REEL CHALLENGE #1

1. A Hard Day's _____ _____ _____ of the Locust
2. Sons and _____ _____ _____ _____ on a Train
3. The _____ _____ _____ in the Afternoon
4. Red _____ _____ _____ _____ of the Jedi
5. Bachelor _____ _____ _____ _____ of
   Frankenstein
6. The Falcon Strikes _____ _____ _____ _____ Cop
7. Love Me _____ _____ _____ _____ of the
   Generals
8. A Patch of _____ _____ Road
9. Gross _____ _____ _____ _____ by Death
10. Pretty _____ _____ _____ Days in May
11. Mr. _____ _____ _____ Passage
12. The L-Shaped _____ _____ _____ _____ Gun
13. It Happened One _____ _____ _____ _____
    _____ Poet's Society
14. Around the World in 80 _____ _____ _____
    Can Wait
15. My Fair _____ _____ _____ _____ Victory

REEL CHALLENGE #2

1. Sea of _____ _____ _____ on the Nile
2. Born _____, _____ _____ _____ Never Comes
3. Two for the _____ _____ _____ Bravo
4. Twelve O'Clock _____ _____ _____ _____ Sky

25

5. Round _____ _____ Delancey

6. Wait Until _____ _____ in the Heart

7. Reflections in a Golden _____ _____ _____ _____ Bay

8. Midnight _____ _____, _____ _____ in My Heart

9. Hester _____ _____ Will Talk

10. The Asphalt _____ _____ of the Year

11. The Lion in _____ _____ in the Piazza

12. So _____ _____ in Mind

13. In Cold _____ _____ Blanket Bingo

14. Thirty Seconds Over _____ _____ Versus the Volcano

15. The Living _____ _____ of the West

REEL CHALLENGE #3

1. True _____ _____ _____ _____ _____ of a Thousand Faces

2. The High and the _____ _____ _____ Guns

3. The Heartbreak _____ _____ Velvet

4. The Art of _____ _____ _____ _____ _____ on Horseback

5. Some Came _____ _____ Stiff

6. Animal _____ _____ _____ Meets the Wolf Man

7. For Your Eyes _____ _____ _____ _____ Misty for Me

8. No Way _____ _____ _____ Screams

9. Raising _____ _____ of the Seven Seas

10. The Great _____ _____ _____ _____
    Correspondent

11. An American in _____, _____ Across the River

12. Black _____, _____ _____ in New York

13. Bright _____ _____ _____ Devils

14. Scream, Pretty _____ _____ _____ _____ to
    the Mob

15. I Love You, _____, _____ _____ Pants

REEL CHALLENGE #4

1. Storm _____ _____ of the Ram

2. The Wicked _____ _____ _____ _____ for Lovers

3. A Blueprint for _____, _____ _____ November

4. Dinner at _____ _____ _____ of the Past

5. Girl _____ _____ _____ Lady

6. Kiss Me _____ _____ When We Meet

7. Imitation of _____ _____ _____ Goose

8. The Last _____ _____ Nights

9. A Little Bit of _____ _____ _____ _____ for a
   Coward

10. The _____ _____ of Souls

11. Carry On _____ _____ _____ _____ Calls

12. Don't Bother to _____ _____ _____ _____-to-Door
    Maniac
13. The _____ _____ of the Line
14. Little Boy _____ _____ _____, America
15. The Gods Must Be _____ _____ of the Wolf

REEL CHALLENGE #5

1. Betsy's _____ _____ _____ Heat
2. Somewhere I'll Find _____ _____ _____
   _____ Letters
3. Middle Age _____ _____ of Cards
4. Joshua Then and _____ _____ _____ and a Day
5. Half Moon _____ _____ Is Magic
6. Murphy's _____ _____ _____ _____ Eyes
7. Somewhere in _____ _____ _____ Bandits
8. The President's _____ _____ _____ _____, Tramp,
   Tramp
9. Lady Be _____ _____ _____ _____ Belt Jones
10. With a Song in My _____ _____ _____ Houses
11. Dying _____ _____ at Gunfight Pass
12. Too Scared to _____ _____ _____ No Evil
13. Fighting _____ _____ Dugan Returns
14. Lovin' _____ _____ _____ _____ Goldfarb, Please
    Come Home
15. Modern _____ _____ _____ _____ of the Sun

REEL CHALLENGE #6

1. I Could Go On _____ _____ for San Sebastian

2. Tobacco _____ _____ _____ Woman

3. Dark _____ _____ _____ _____ Be My Destiny

4. Postcards from the _____ _____ _____
   _____ Limits

5. Sentimental _____ _____ _____ of Day

6. A Lovely Way to _____ _____, Fast and Beautiful

7. The Incredible Lightness of _____ _____ Was a
   Crooked Man

8. The Devil's _____ _____ with a Million

9. She's Gotta Have _____ _____ _____ _____
   _____ _____ Wind to Java

10. Life Begins at _____ _____ _____ _____ in Mind

11. The Secret _____ _____ _____ _____ and Let Die

12. Sam's _____ _____ _____, King of the Monsters

13. Hit the _____ _____ _____ in the Kitchen

14. The Ox-Bow _____ _____ _____ Cowboy

15. I Am Curious _____ _____ Patrol

REEL CHALLENGE #7

1. Magnum _____ : _____ Easy Pieces

2. The Macomber _____ _____ _____ _____ in
   My Arms

29

3. Lust for _____ _____ of the Lost Ark

4. Something _____ _____ _____ _____ Across the Everglades

5. The Last American _____ _____ _____ _____ Train

6. Troop Beverly _____ _____ _____ of the Brave

7. Duet for _____ _____ _____ _____ or Be Killed

8. Foul _____ _____ Dingus Magee

9. A Touch of _____ _____ Jackson

10. Earth Girls Are _____ _____ _____ at First Bite

11. The Devil's _____ _____ _____ on the Wild Side

12. Dirty Little _____ _____ _____ Galahad

13. Four Rode _____ _____ _____ _____ Without End

14. Hearts of the _____ _____ _____ of a Woman

15. And Then There Were _____ _____ _____ _____ _____ Like a Wheel

HALF & HALF

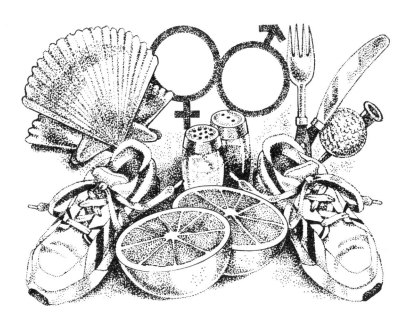

General Instructions

In each of the following games, 64 squares are found in a grid. Each square contains three letters that make up either the first or last half of a six-letter word. The other half of the word can also be found in the grid. The completed puzzle will list 32 six-letter words. We've done the first word to get you started.

HALF & HALF #1

MAN	ONE	EXP	EXH	TEM	NER	CUE	HAZ
RRY	ACC	HIJ	VER	ATT	BEG	IST	TER
SIS	THR	ASP	GAR	HOM	POE	KLE	ECT
SPE	PLE	OSE	BLA	HID	GOS	VER	ECH
DIN	SHI	REM	BAL	TRY	PIC	FOU	ARD
ALE	PAN	ENL	INY	UAL	END	DON	ORC
HIN	OST	FLO	URC	QUA	TOR	TIC	ATE
ACK	NCH	PEL	EDY	RID	QUE	FES	GHT

1. _____Accost_____ 12. _____ 23. _____
2. _____ 13. _____ 24. _____
3. _____ 14. _____ 25. _____
4. _____ 15. _____ 26. _____
5. _____ 16. _____ 27. _____
6. _____ 17. _____ 28. _____
7. _____ 18. _____ 29. _____
8. _____ 19. _____ 30. _____
9. _____ 20. _____ 31. _____
10. _____ 21. _____ 32. _____
11. _____ 22. _____

HALF & HALF #2

ABR	ERS	EAM	SON	INO	TED	TTY	ILL
WAR	SIS	NUM	TTO	UNI	URE	ATZ	CET
DOM	BLE	WHI	UNA	REN	LIN	THR	UPT
GEY	PER	INI	TON	AGE	PRE	HER	MSY
RAI	VIC	NTY	ABJ	FAT	CAN	VAN	COU
ATE	TEX	SIL	ARD	DAL	THE	MAR	FEE
SER	SCR	GHE	ANI	DUE	MAL	DUL	TYR
VOR	SIN	MIT	BER	OPI	IUM	NNA	BIK

1. _____Abjure_____   12. _____   23. _____
2. _____   13. _____   24. _____
3. _____   14. _____   25. _____
4. _____   15. _____   26. _____
5. _____   16. _____   27. _____
6. _____   17. _____   28. _____
7. _____   18. _____   29. _____
8. _____   19. _____   30. _____
9. _____   20. _____   31. _____
10. _____   21. _____   32. _____
11. _____   22. _____

HALF & HALF #3

KIS	PEN	MAD	ANT	RES	DIA	IPE	OLL
MIR	ANI	REC	EFF	ROR	RUF	ORD	WSE
RAS	IGY	HOP	INT	FIX	PLE	UAL	WNY
ARY	SCO	ORT	BRO	AND	OXF	FLE	REE
BIS	BRA	SEN	DGE	BLE	CLE	CON	GAM
TCH	ULT	VEL	MET	EST	MUT	DEG	ISL
ONE	BEH	PRE	HEM	TRA	FAL	BAT	MUS
MUS	PLE	PEO	TEN	LAW	PER	SCR	YER

1. _____Animus_____   12. _____   23. _____
2. _____   13. _____   24. _____
3. _____   14. _____   25. _____
4. _____   15. _____   26. _____
5. _____   16. _____   27. _____
6. _____   17. _____   28. _____
7. _____   18. _____   29. _____
8. _____   19. _____   30. _____
9. _____   20. _____   31. _____
10. _____   21. _____   32. _____
11. _____   22. _____

HALF & HALF #4

JUN	TRE	TON	DER	VET	PAD	MOR	VAN
VER	ATE	NAL	NCH	REA	REC	MIN	OCE
FIN	TIC	RUS	CLA	BRI	VER	PEW	UME
MOR	NOU	TER	ORY	DAL	CRU	ARY	KET
BIT	ATY	DEN	GAT	WEA	GUE	SEL	VEL
TLE	RAB	MUT	NOT	ENT	EFT	DLE	SKY
SAV	MYS	GER	UPD	LOT	ITY	VOL	EDE
TAL	BET	BER	TEN	SON	BUR	WHI	GOB

1. ___Bereft___
2. _____
3. _____
4. _____
5. _____
6. _____
7. _____
8. _____
9. _____
10. _____
11. _____
12. _____
13. _____
14. _____
15. _____
16. _____
17. _____
18. _____
19. _____
20. _____
21. _____
22. _____
23. _____
24. _____
25. _____
26. _____
27. _____
28. _____
29. _____
30. _____
31. _____
32. _____

HALF & HALF #5

HEI	CUS	PUR	ENT	FRU	MON	DUE	OKE
DAM	BOL	ILE	ASK	LEX	OYS	NUM	JOV
BRA	ZEA	CIR	REV	PET	GHT	ETY	SUB
ISM	LOT	DEP	TLE	SUF	MAG	VEN	GAI
COS	GAM	LOW	HEA	VEN	SPA	GON	LAP
REL	ACH	PRE	ITE	GAL	TER	FUT	FIX
UTY	NDY	REF	YEL	VEL	KNI	FER	PLE
MOS	IGN	VIN	JAR	PAR	LUM	IAL	ODY

1.	Brandy	12.	_____	23.	_____
2.	_____	13.	_____	24.	_____
3.	_____	14.	_____	25.	_____
4.	_____	15.	_____	26.	_____
5.	_____	16.	_____	27.	_____
6.	_____	17.	_____	28.	_____
7.	_____	18.	_____	29.	_____
8.	_____	19.	_____	30.	_____
9.	_____	20.	_____	31.	_____
10.	_____	21.	_____	32.	_____
11.	_____	22.	_____		

HALF & HALF #6

EXP	TAB	BLI	NCH	CRO	ISE	ECT	POO
CLE	TEM	BER	RIC	BOO	LAP	IAN	ITY
MAR	CIR	PIR	BUT	BAL	FOS	MEL	SLO
MED	LAU	RCH	OUS	GAN	INE	BLE	RUB
ARD	BAM	SYS	SAN	VER	BRA	RCE	LET
GEN	ACY	FAC	GHT	ILE	TLE	CLO	BUR
CAT	IBI	LIM	UCH	ODY	SOU	DLE	TON
DEM	IAL	ENG	STA	POR	TER	VIO	SAM

1.	Balsam	12.	_____	23.	_____
2.	_____	13.	_____	24.	_____
3.	_____	14.	_____	25.	_____
4.	_____	15.	_____	26.	_____
5.	_____	16.	_____	27.	_____
6.	_____	17.	_____	28.	_____
7.	_____	18.	_____	29.	_____
8.	_____	19.	_____	30.	_____
9.	_____	20.	_____	31.	_____
10.	_____	21.	_____	32.	_____
11.	_____	22.	_____		

HALF & HALF #7

SIM	ORE	QUA	MUS	LET	NET	ROT	ION
ERN	SIP	FED	EQU	HAR	RAD	VER	THE
IAL	KET	GRO	MSY	UDE	LIN	LEN	VOY
ZOD	IGN	IAC	GOB	IOR	PLA	SCA	SIL
ALL	INT	GTH	INE	PIC	PAL	KLE	LES
WYV	ORA	LIT	SEN	SCE	TIC	BAR	FLI
FOI	HON	ROW	NIC	EUR	QUI	FOS	BLE
LAR	PRA	YER	UCH	PLE	ISO	PIL	UND

1. _____Allude_____
2. _____
3. _____
4. _____
5. _____
6. _____
7. _____
8. _____
9. _____
10. _____
11. _____
12. _____
13. _____
14. _____
15. _____
16. _____
17. _____
18. _____
19. _____
20. _____
21. _____
22. _____
23. _____
24. _____
25. _____
26. _____
27. _____
28. _____
29. _____
30. _____
31. _____
32. _____

CHAIN LETTERS

General Instructions

These puzzles challenge you to correctly complete the words across in each grid in order to discover the missing vertical word pertaining to the puzzle category. Words across may have more than a single solution, but only one is correct. Making the right connection is the key!

CHAIN LETTERS #1
Traveller's Advisory

Three natural disasters await you in the grids below. Correctly complete the words across so that the boxes, when read from top to bottom, will spell the danger to be avoided.

```
A C [ ] E D      D I [ ] T Y      S P [ ] T E
F L [ ] N G      T R [ ] C K      R E [ ] E L
C A [ ] E S      N O [ ] E S      B R [ ] W N
F E [ ] A L      W H [ ] L E      T I [ ] T S
S T [ ] L E      M A [ ] L S      G L [ ] S S
D A [ ] E S      C O [ ] E R      P I [ ] E D
D R [ ] N K      B R [ ] S H      R I [ ] E R
I N [ ] E R      L O [ ] E R      O T [ ] E R
B L [ ] N D      S T [ ] L E      F L [ ] C K
```

CHAIN LETTERS #2
A Musical Note

In the grids below, three renowned international composers can be found. Their names will be revealed in the boxes from top to bottom when you correctly complete the words across.

```
U M [ ] R A      B O [ ] E Y      L O [ ] A R
C H [ ] W Y      T R [ ] E S      B R [ ] A D
E R [ ] I E      J E [ ] K Y      S L [ ] E K
T E [ ] E T      A R [ ] O N      E X [ ] O L
B I [ ] O N      I C [ ] O R      O C [ ] E R
L A [ ] E X      T A [ ] N Y      G R [ ] S S
B E [ ] R Y      D R [ ] V E      E N [ ] O Y
A L [ ] G N      L O [ ] E R      S P [ ] N T
R I [ ] G S                       T I [ ] E S
```

38

CHAIN LETTERS #3
When You Wish Upon a Star

The names of three constellations viewed from the Earth can be found below in the boxes, from top to bottom. Complete the words across with the correct letter and see stars!

B	L		N	D		P	A		R	Y		L	Y		E	E
D	E		I	M		T	H		M	E		B	L		A	T
L	O		E	N		P	E		A	L		M	A		O	R
D	O		T	Y		T	R		B	E		D	E		E	R
W	R		N	G		C	Y		L	E		C	O		C	H
N	Y		P	H		S	T		N	T		S	K		L	L
B	R		V	E		P	I		O	T		S	P		I	G
C	I		E	R		C	L		C	K		T	R		N	K
S	H		R	E		L	I		B	O		C	A		T	E

CHAIN LETTERS #4
Lights, Camera, Action

Hidden in the boxes below, from top to bottom, are the names of three of the movie industry's top directors. These Oscar winners can be found by completing the words across with the correct letter.

B	I		L	E		D	E		O	N		P	A		T	Y
W	E		D	Y		C	R		F	T		G	U		D	E
H	E		O	N		M	O		E	Y		P	I		O	T
U	L		R	A		B	A		E	R		W	A		O	O
W	R		N	G		F	E		N	T		F	L		M	E
J	U		E	P		S	H		I	K		P	U		G	E
F	A		N	A		J	E		E	L		C	E		A	R
D	U		K	Y		A	M		T	Y		H	U		S	Y
Y	A		H	T		N	I		H	E		G	R		V	E
M	A		Z	E		M	E		Z	O		C	O		G	O

CHAIN LETTERS #5
Let the Games Begin

The Olympic Games are held at different locales around the world. Below you'll find three sites of past competitions—just correctly fill in the words across and the answers will be revealed.

T	H		N	K
D	I		E	R
F	A		C	Y
B	O		O	M
E	L		O	W
L	A		G	E
C	R		M	B
L	O		K	S
W	A		E	N

L	A		E	R
D	I		G	E
F	L		S	H
V	E		U	E
S	C		N	E
I	M		E	D
E	C		A	T
C	L		A	N

D	E		U	R
D	U		L	S
D	O		L	Y
E	M		A	R
P	E		N	Y
B	L		R	B
T	I		E	D
D	I		G	O
A	R		N	A

CHAIN LETTERS #6
Native Americans

The names of three Indian tribes can be found hidden in the grids below. The tribal names can be found by correctly filling in the words across—the answers will be revealed in the squares from top to bottom.

L	O		E	R
P	E		R	S
L	U		P	S
Q	U		T	E
C	O		E	S
S	P		I	L
M	A		E	S
R	E		V	E

C	H		C	K
M	A		C	H
G	R		V	E
T	O		U	E
P	L		M	S
W	O		D	S
C	R		M	P
R	E		T	S

P	O		E	S
G	R		N	D
B	U		K	S
L	A		E	S
C	L		P	S
T	A		E	S
B	R		K	E
P	R		U	D

MISSING LINKS

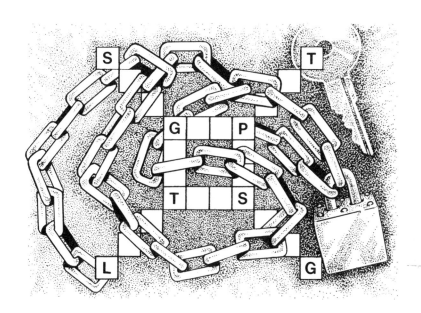

General Instructions

In the puzzles that follow, fill in the blanks so that each line of four letters spells a word forward and backwards. Example: __TO__ can be completed with an S and a P to spell STOP in one direction and POTS in the other.

MISSING LINKS #1

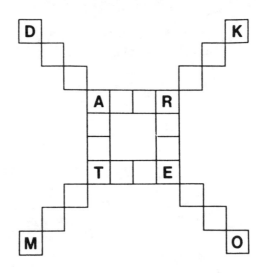

MISSING LINKS #2

MISSING LINKS #3

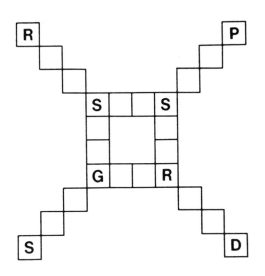

MISSING LINKS #4

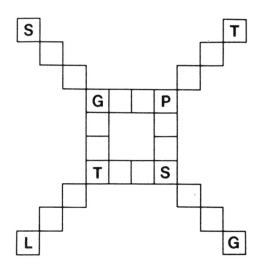

MISSING LINKS #5

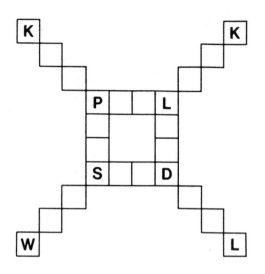

MISSING LINKS #6

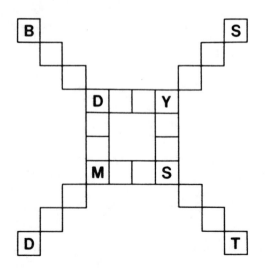

44

MISSING LINKS #7

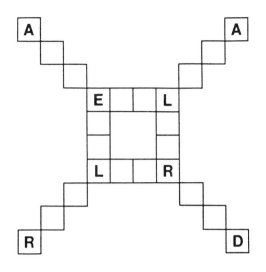

QUOTABLES

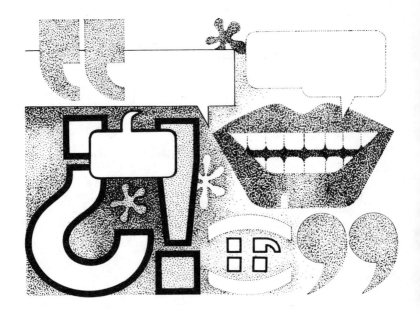

General Instructions

Test your knowledge of past and present, and the people who have made them both more memorable through words. The following puzzles ask you to match some quotes with the people who said them, but remember—this task may be easier said than done!

QUOTABLES #1
A Topical Garden

1. "Knowledge and human power are synonymous."
   A. William Randolph Hearst
   B. Francis Bacon
   C. Henry Kissinger
   D. Winston Churchill

2. "Truth is its own reward."
   A. Benjamin Disraeli
   B. William Shakespeare
   C. Plato
   D. Ralph Waldo Emerson

3. "Ability is nothing without opportunity."
   A. Napoleon
   B. John F. Kennedy
   C. Henry Ford
   D. Rev. Jesse Jackson

4. "It matters not how a man dies, but how he lives."
   A. Anne Frank
   B. Eleanor Roosevelt
   C. Charles Dickens
   D. Samuel Johnson

5. "If fifty million people say a foolish thing it is still a foolish thing."
   A. George Gallup
   B. Anatole France
   C. Harry S. Truman
   D. Will Rogers

6. "Experience . . . is simply the name we give our mistakes."
   A. Alan Watts
   B. Tennessee Williams
   C. Aldous Huxley
   D. Oscar Wilde

7. "After all there is but one race—humanity."
   A. Abraham Lincoln

B. Martin Luther King, Jr.
C. George Moore
D. Robert F. Kennedy

8. "Absence makes the heart grow fonder."
    A. Percy Bysshe Shelley
    B. Thomas Haynes Bayly
    C. Elizabeth Barrett Browning
    D. Emily Dickinson

9. "Virtue has never been as respected as money."
    A. John Kenneth Galbraith
    B. Donald Trump
    C. Mark Twain
    D. Ted Turner

10. "Imagination is more important than knowledge."
    A. Albert Einstein
    B. Pablo Picasso
    C. Kurt Vonnegut
    D. Malcolm Forbes

QUOTABLES #2
On the Heir

1. "Parents can only give good advice or put them on the right paths, but the final forming of a person's character lies in their own hands."
    A. Anne Frank
    B. Ralph Waldo Emerson
    C. Marguerite Kelly
    D. Eda J. LeShan

2. "In the final analysis it is not what you do for your children but what you have taught them to do for themselves that will make them successful human beings."
    A. Robert Fulghum
    B. Ann Landers
    C. Dr. Terry Brazelton
    D. Franklin P. Jones

3. "Parents of young children should realize that few people, and maybe no one, will find their children as enchanting as they do."
   A. Dave Barry
   B. Erma Bombeck
   C. Jean Kerr
   D. Barbara Walters

4. "Children are the keys to paradise."
   A. R. H. Stoddard
   B. Fred Rogers
   C. Laura Ashley
   D. Erich Segal

5. "Childhood is frequently a solemn business for those inside it."
   A. Maya Angelou
   B. George Will
   C. Oprah Winfrey
   D. Abigail Van Buren

6. "By giving children lots of affection, you can help fill them with love and acceptance of themselves. Then that's what they will have to give away."
   A. Susan Castro
   B. Jim Henson
   C. Dr. Wayne Dyer
   D. Jill Ireland

7. "Today's children are the first generation to grow up in a world that has the power to destroy itself."
   A. Rachel Carson
   B. Margaret Mead
   C. Garry Trudeau
   D. Stanley Winger

8. "If help and salvation are to come, they can only come from the children, for the children are the makers of men."
   A. Eda J. LeShan
   B. John Updike
   C. Isaac Singer
   D. Maria Montessori

9. "Children are educated by what the grownup is and not by his talk."
   A. Carl Jung
   B. Raymond Walters
   C. Walt Whitman
   D. Sigmund Freud

10. "The best brought-up children are those who have seen their parents as they are. Hypocrisy is not the parent's first duty."
    A. Gerald Ford
    B. Charles Dickens
    C. George Bernard Shaw
    D. Cher

QUOTABLES #3

Love Notes

1. "Love is not enough. It must be the foundation, the cornerstone—but not the complete structure. It is much too pliable, too yielding."
   A. Ingrid Bergman
   B. Percy Wallingford
   C. Erica Jong
   D. Bette Davis

2. "There is only one happiness in life, to love and be loved."
   A. William Shakespeare
   B. George Sand
   C. Elizabeth Barrett Browning
   D. Barbara Cartland

3. "The giving of love is an education in itself."
   A. Eleanor Roosevelt
   B. Mother Teresa
   C. Werner Erhard
   D. Adela Rogers St. John

4. "Love is the triumph of imagination over intelligence."
   A. Norman Mailer

B. H. L. Mencken
C. Lillian Hellman
D. Nora Ephron

5. "Love is but the discovery of ourselves in others, and the delight in the recognition."
   A. F. Scott Fitzgerald
   B. Judith Viorst
   C. Alexander Smith
   D. Martin Abraham

6. "Love is the greatest refreshment in life."
   A. Pablo Picasso
   B. Sylvia Plath
   C. Martha Stewart
   D. Maria Callas

7. "Life has taught us that love does not consist in gazing at each other but in looking outward together in the same direction."
   A. Anaïs Nin
   B. Richard Bach
   C. Janet Dailey
   D. Antoine de Saint-Exupéry

8. "Love is an irresistible desire to be irresistibly desired."
   A. Mary Pickford
   B. Robert Frost
   C. Danielle Steel
   D. Dorothy Parker

9. "The best proof of love is trust."
   A. Dr. Joyce Brothers
   B. Leo Buscaglia
   C. Jane Austen
   D. Charles Dickens

10. "Among those whom I admire, I can find no common denominator, but among those whom I love, I can: all of them make me laugh."
    A. J. P. Morgan
    B. Barbara Walters
    C. W. H. Auden
    D. Cole Porter

QUOTABLES #4

The Ties That Bind

1. "[Marriage] can be compared to a cage: birds outside it despair to enter, and birds within, to escape."
   A. Alexandre Dumas
   B. Montaigne
   C. Charles Baudelaire
   D. Marcel Proust

2. "If married couples did not live together, happy marriages would be more frequent."
   A. John Huston
   B. James Bell
   C. Nietzsche
   D. Marvin Mitchelson

3. "Marriage must incessantly contend with a monster that devours everything: familiarity."
   A. Louis Malle
   B. Hugh Hefner
   C. Gloria Vanderbilt
   D. Balzac

4. "Marriages are made in Heaven."
   A. Voltaire
   B. Alfred Tennyson
   C. Louisa May Alcott
   D. Anatole France

5. "Marriage is neither Heaven nor Hell; it is simply purgatory."
   A. Abraham Lincoln
   B. Louis L'Amour
   C. Joyce Carol Oates
   D. August Strindberg

6. "Only choose in marriage a woman whom you would choose as a friend if she were a man."
   A. Clark Gable
   B. Joseph Joubert

    C. Maurice Chevalier
    D. Gregory Peck

7. "Marriage is a bargain, and somebody has to get the worst of the bargain."
    A. Judith Viorst
    B. Melvin Belli
    C. Helen Rowland
    D. Joanne Woodward

8. "The surest way to be alone is to get married."
    A. Gloria Steinem
    B. Ava Gardner
    C. Elizabeth Taylor
    D. Cary Grant

9. "Marriage resembles a pair of shears, so joined that they cannot be separated; often moving in opposite directions, yet always punishing anyone who comes between them."
    A. Leona Helmsley
    B. Helen Gurley Brown
    C. Felice Casorati
    D. Sidney Smith

10. "Marriage is the only adventure open to the cowardly."
    A. Lewis Grizzard
    B. Johnny Carson
    C. Voltaire
    D. Truman Capote

QUOTABLES #5

Golden Years

1. "None are so old as those who have outlived enthusiasm."
    A. Henry David Thoreau
    B. Martha Graham
    C. Helen Hayes
    D. Dizzy Gillespie

8. "You can't help getting older but you don't have to get old."
    A. George Burns
    B. Chic Young
    C. Gene Kelly
    D. George Balanchine

9. "Just remember, once you're over the hill you begin to pick up speed."
    A. Jim Burlington
    B. Darryl Zanuck
    C. Charles Schultz
    D. Hermes Pan

10. "If a thing is old, it is a sign that it was fit to live. The guarantee of continuity is quality."
    A. Paul Foxworth
    B. Eddie Rickenbacker
    C. Albert Einstein
    D. Barry Levinson

QUOTABLES #6

Character Studies

1. "You have to accept whatever comes and the important thing is that you meet it with courage and with the best that you have to give."
    A. Rose Kennedy
    B. Eleanor Roosevelt
    C. Leo C. Rosten
    D. Spencer Tracy

2. "When we can begin to take our failures nonseriously, it means we are ceasing to be afraid of them. It is of immense importance to learn to laugh at ourselves."
    A. Katherine Mansfield
    B. Art Buchwald
    C. Sally Jessy Raphael
    D. Armand Hammer

3. "Let the world know you as you are, not as you think you

should be, because sooner or later, if you are posing, you will forget the pose, and then where are you?"
A. Millicent Fenwick
B. Andy Rooney
C. Jimmy Stewart
D. Fanny Brice

4. "Champions take responsibility. When the ball is coming over the net, you can be sure I want the ball."
A. Billie Jean King
B. Michael Eisner
C. Rupert Murdoch
D. Arthur Ashe

5. "There's right and there's wrong. You get to do one or the other. You do the one, and you're living. You do the other, and you may be walking around but you're dead as a beaver hat."
A. Larry McMurtry
B. Will Rogers
C. John Wayne
D. Nolan Ryan

6. "The only causes of regret are laziness, outbursts of temper, hurting others, prejudice, jealousy and envy."
A. Louis Sullivan
B. Germaine Greer
C. Elizabeth Dole
D. O. Henry

7. "The quality of strength lined with tenderness is an unbeatable combination, as are intelligence and necessity when unblunted by formal education."
A. Mark Matha Bane
B. Maya Angelou
C. J. D. Salinger
D. Benjamin Hooks

8. "You can't give people pride, but you can provide the kind of understanding that makes people look to their inner strengths and find their own sense of pride."
A. Harry S. Truman
B. Nelson Mandela

C. Eunice Shriver
D. Charleszetta Waddles

9. "The measure of a man's real character is what he would do if he knew he would never be found out."
A. Thomas Jefferson
B. Macaulay
C. Benjamin Franklin
D. George Washington

10. "We often pray for purity, unselfishness, for the highest qualities of character, and forget that these things cannot be given, but must be earned."
A. Rev. Billy Graham
B. Eliot Porter
C. Lymon Abbott
D. Balzac

QUOTABLES #7
Nothing Succeeds Like . . .

1. "Experience shows that success is due less to ability than to zeal. The winner is he who gives himself to his work, body and soul."
A. Jeffrey Katzenburg
B. John Glenn
C. Charles Buxton
D. Henry Freeman

2. "Those who dare to fail miserably can achieve greatly."
A. I. M. Pei
B. Benjamin Bradlee
C. Richard Byrd
D. Robert F. Kennedy

3. "The man who will use his skill and constructive imagination to see how much he can give for a dollar, instead of how little he can give for a dollar, is bound to succeed."
A. Henry Ford

B. Sam Walton
C. Charles Revson
D. F. W. Woolworth

4. "Success follows doing what you want to do. There is no other way to be successful."
A. Bill Cosby
B. Helen Frankenthaler
C. Malcolm Forbes
D. Warren Beatty

5. "These three things—work, will, success—fill human existences. Will opens the door to success, both brilliant and happy. Work passes these doors, and at the end of the journey success comes in to crown one's efforts."
A. Charles Lindbergh
B. Jonas Salk
C. Lee Iacocca
D. Louis Pasteur

6. "There is only one success—to be able to spend your life in your own way."
A. Mark Goodson
B. Christopher Morley
C. Charles Yeager
D. David Geffen

7. "The man who wins may have been counted out several times, but he didn't hear the referee."
A. A. J. Foyt
B. Jim Bakker
C. H. E. Hansen
D. Greg LeMond

8. "A great business success was probably never attained by chasing the dollar, but is due to pride in one's work—the pride that makes business an art."
A. Jack Robinson
B. Henry L. Doherty
C. M. C. Mitchell
D. Harry Reasoner

9. "The three great essentials to achieve anything worthwhile are, first, hard work; second, stick-to-itiveness;

third, common sense."
A. Thomas A. Edison
B. James Grant
C. Eileen Ford
D. Robert Sanger

10. "If you want to succeed, you should strike out on new paths rather than travel the worn paths of accepted success."
A. Arnold Schwarzenegger
B. William S. Paley
C. Christian Barnard
D. John D. Rockefeller

NOW YOU SEE IT

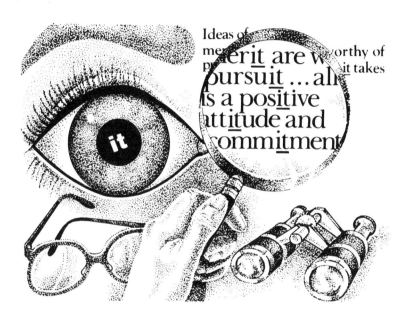

Ideas of merit are worthy of pursuit ... all it takes is a positive attitude and commitment

General Instructions

Camouflaged in the following stories are many hidden words pertaining to the chosen category. Search for them within and between the words, and reading between the lines may be helpful! We've underlined the first one to get you started.

NOW YOU SEE IT #1

Colors are the name of the game in the puzzle below. Super sleuths will find 18 colors hidden within the story.

Room for Improvement

"I'm tired of the rattan furniture in this room, Oscar—let's try a new look," Rose said. "Perhaps a quaint country motif or a period look with fetching old accent pieces. Do you agree?" "No," Oscar replied. "I like what we've got."

"Well, I'm extremely impressed by your open mind," Rose answered, her brow nastily arching. "I trust this means we can't even discuss it?"

"Why should we?" he shrugged. "You always win every so-called discussion we have, anyway. And neither your intimidation nor anger is going to change my mind. Get my message?"

Rose resorted to her oldest trick: flattery. "I should be nicer, I see that now. But I hate all these big decisions. And you do have excellent taste."

"Well-l-l," Oscar capitulated. "Maybe I did overreact. Just do whatever you like. Your choice of decor always pleases me."

"Why, Oscar, you're the most romantic fool I've ever known," Rose gushed, and immediately called her decorator.

NOW YOU SEE IT #2

Only the sharpest eye will detect all of the 27 creatures hidden in the story below.

Survival of the Fittest

It was his first agonizing day on the job, and the new entertainment director at the retirement center ate little during lunch.

"I'm afraid the kayak excursion will be entirely too strenuous for these senior citizens," he fretted to himself, pushing his plate aside while fishing for the aspirin tin in his pocket. "And what if they're not terribly fond of scuba diving or water volleyball, either?"

He swallowed hard, scowling as he realized there wasn't one land activity in which he could confidently supervise them unless, he thought suddenly, they liked bowling. Of course! The idea of bowling was perfectly brilliant—a great way to stay in shape and share a group activity, too!

But when the young director proposed they have a go at it, the seniors groused loudly. "Bowling is out of the question, you overbearing nuisance," declared one. "Training for the Olympic Decathlon demands quite enough of our time, thank you!"

NOW YOU SEE IT #3

Common items found in almost every household abound in the following story. Although carefully concealed, a close check of every nook and cranny will reveal 26!

Looking Out for Number One

Eva seemed quieter than usual, Arthur thought. She wasn't very animated, and even that chic hairdo she'd had Ivan give her yesterday was now limp and drab.

When asked how she felt, Eva appeared to welcome the attention. "My head aches terribly," she fretted, "and I feel so faint. Forgive me for moping around like this."

"Let's hop in the car, pet, and take you to see Dr. Apelgren," Arthur said. "He can prescribe some drugs to help you. But we should be doing something now—not later."

"Relax, dear," said Eva. "There's no need to get the least overwrought. But," she added, giving him a mock rap on his chin, "any ailing lass would be bowled over by such attentiveness."

Arthur was too embarrassed to tell her that he'd actually been thinking, "If I don't keep Eva's health stable, then who'll take care of me?" So he simply replied, with hardly a trace of irony in his voice, "Any husband worth his salt would do the same, love!"

NOW YOU SEE IT #4

You're just a stone's throw from 13 kinds of rocks hidden beneath the surface of the story below. Once again, finding each formation is the key!

The Art of the Short Story

Entering through a gate in back, Opal Emery caught her two grandchildren totally by surprise. As they ran to her, she headed for the porch swing, saying, "Okay—last one on my lap is a rotten egg!"

"Sticks and stones may break my bones, but names can never hurt me," they chimed in unison, as each pounced on an empty knee.

"Will you tell us a story?" asked Ruby, the older child.

"Not unless Hale stops squirming," Opal replied, with a jaded glance at her grandson. He smiled shyly and snuggled closer, savoring the smell of the talcum his grandmother always wore. Then he sneezed, his nose tickled by an unseen piece of lint in the air.

"Bless you," Opal said, then she began. "Since it's late, I'll tell you a tale my first teacher told me—a very short ghost story, as I recall," she said slyly, "about a ghost who was simply too short to be the subject of a tall tale." And on that note, she arose and left.

"That Gran—I tell you, she's a card," said Ruby, watching her depart.

"One who should be dealt with!" Hale grinned, repeating one of Opal's favorite puns. Laughing, they resumed playing.

NOW YOU SEE IT #5

Successfully complete this puzzle by finding 27 wearable items strewn around in the story maze below.

Ducking the Issue

Dickie Chatham took umbrage at his school's mascot: a duck! Seething, he wondered which dumb louses had suggested such a name, and how the situation could best be addressed.

He'd go right to the top, Dickie decided. He'd just find the courage and stamina to talk to the principal and make short shrift of the matter. The outcome was inescapable—a new mascot would be chosen by the student body.

Sashaying into the principal's office, he explained his purpose. "Oh, pshaw," lisped the secretary, Jean Smithers, through her braces. "He's never in during the mornings, but he'll be returning this afternoon."

Through the window behind her, Dickie was watching as the principal's car flashed by. Following his gaze, she said, "He's early! No sweat, sir—I'll get you in right away."

After the meeting, Dickie felt defeated. The principal, haughtier than ever, had refused to give the idea even minimum consideration. Pursing his lips and with no vestige of warmth, he recited the school's motto instead: "If it's your luck to be a duck, then never, ever run amuck; just stay the course and mark my word—you'll always be the early bird!"

Dickie never forgot. After graduation he entered medical school, and became a very wealthy quack.

NOW YOU SEE IT #6

If you have an appetite for the obscure, you should fare very well with this puzzle. A combination plate of 18 fruits and vegetables awaits you.

Ordering à la Carte

"It appears that my friend, Allen Tilton, has set a date for his one-man art show," Cornelia Green said, smiling at her handsome male secretary, "and nothing will appease him if I don't attend. So be a nice fellow and cancel my trip to San Antonio next week, Alex."

"That won't take me long," he replied. "Anything else?"

"Yes. You escort me to the show, and in return, I promote you to administrative assistant."

"You're very generous," Alex said, and as he studied her sleek demeanor, anger washed over him. "But why would you promote me?"

"Because I don't socialize with mere secretaries!"

"I never figured you for such a snob," Alex shot back. "Now that I know what a witch I've been working for, you can have your job back!"

"It may amuse you to know that I'd hoped for this reaction," Cornelia smiled. "Now we can see each other without my having to worry about dating an employee!"

"Not in this lifetime," Alex said, "and not in Tilton's, either. Every time I see his so-called art, I choke!"

A week later, Cornelia forgot all about Alex when the receptionist buzzed her on the intercom to say, "Your new secretary, Brad, is here . . . will that be two for lunch?"

NOW YOU SEE IT #7

In this story, locate 24 toys, objects, or games associated with children's recreation and entertainment. Ready, set, go!

First Things First

Jack's mom, Dolly Glover, was always on the ball where her son was concerned. She cared deeply about his welfare and giving him a proper education, constantly drumming into his head, "Carouse less and study more, don't let important things slide, plan every move before you jump, and always remember—books are your friends!"

Jack found it hard to mask his impatience with her prattle and dogma. They struck him as unnecessary, and he wished she'd stop lecturing him.

He was more at home with a hoop and, given a ball, could slam-dunk it every time. So sure was he of a pro career, in fact, that Jack didn't even intend or aspire to graduate.

When Dolly found out, the lines of battle were drawn. She grounded Jack until he finished college five years later and signed with the team of his choice.

A multimillionaire when he retired, Jack attributed his success to his mother. "She's the best friend and most worthy opponent I've ever had," he said, "and she never even got called for goal tending!"

SPELLBINDERS

General Instructions

Each of the following games contains two groups of letters. Each group, when properly arranged, spells five common words. Following the example below, rearrange the letters displayed beside each grid and list your answers in the spaces provided. (The example calls for only three words.)

"A-E-C-M"

C	A	M	E
M	A	C	E
A	C	M	E

SPELLBINDERS #1

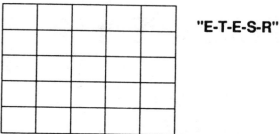

"E-T-E-S-R"

"R-I-T-P-S-E"

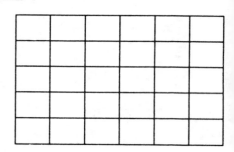

SPELLBINDERS #2

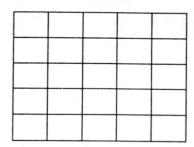

"L-S-E-T-A"

"S-R-T-A-C-E"

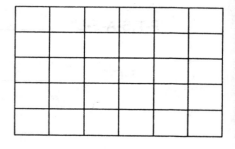

SPELLBINDERS #3

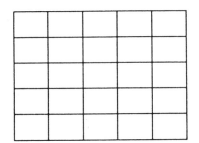
"A-R-S-P-E"

"W-E-R-R-A-D"
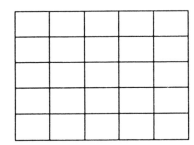

SPELLBINDERS #4

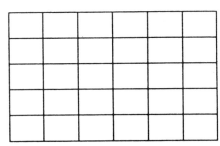
"E-B-T-A-S"

"P-T-S-A-E-L"
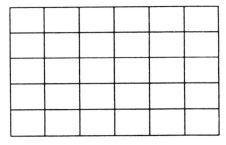

SPELLBINDERS #5

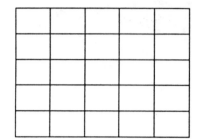

"P-S-L-A-E"

"V-L-E-S-R-A"

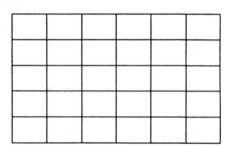

SPELLBINDERS #6

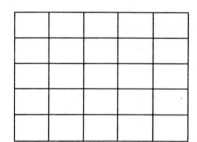

"N-T-O-S-E"

"T-C-A-R-E-N"

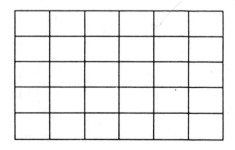

SPELLBINDERS #7

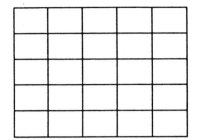

"I-E-S-N-R"

"I-M-T-E-S-R"

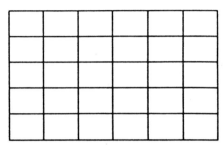

MYSTERY MAZE

General Instructions

In the following letter mazes, you'll find hidden names pertaining to the chosen category. Find the names by linking adjoining letters in the proper sequence—no skipping allowed! Letters may join vertically, diagonally, or horizontally in any direction, but the same letter may not be used more than once in any answer.

70

MYSTERY MAZE #1

Foreign Exchange

Below you'll find names of 12 currencies used in countries around the world. Find them and you'll be in the money!

L	I	U	K	N
E	P	R	A	D
E	L	O	N	I
O	S	U	A	E
C	Y	C	R	Y

MYSTERY MAZE #2

Star Search

Do you believe that the stars influence your life? Below you'll find seven astrological signs—are you destined to find yours?

A	U	G	E	S
T	R	B	O	C
N	I	U	S	R
L	V	E	P	I
E	O	I	C	V

MYSTERY MAZE #3

Strike Up the Band

They'll be playing your song if you can identify the seven musical instruments in the maze below.

F	C	O	H	E
T	L	A	B	O
P	R	U	L	L
I	T	E	M	I
E	N	C	P	O

MYSTERY MAZE #4

Herbs

Culinary experts will recognize the seven herbs in the puzzle below as the finishing touches to some tasty dishes!

M	C	R	D	L
A	S	O	I	L
P	R	N	S	M
E	T	J	A	G
P	O	R	E	B

MYSTERY MAZE #5

Hook, Line, and Sinker

Fish through the puzzle below to hook your favorite catch of the day. Nine answers await—"water" you waiting for?

S	R	I	M	P
H	D	D	B	U
A	L	I	O	T
N	U	R	C	O
S	T	A	B	K

MYSTERY MAZE #6

A Flavorful Medley

Variety may be the spice of life, but the six ingredients hidden below can also be counted on to add some flavor!

P	L	M	U	C
A	E	L	I	N
N	P	R	K	A
I	P	E	V	C
M	S	C	O	L

MYSTERY MAZE #7
What's Up, Doc?

Diamonds may be a girl's best friend, but they're not the only "carats" that will catch your eye in the puzzle below . . . six gemstones are included.

H	E	R	A	C
D	O	M	T	I
U	N	E	O	D
B	R	P	L	A
Y	Z	A	G	F

ANSWERS

CIRCLE SEARCH

#1, All in a Day's Work

```
R E C N A D s M U S I C I A N
E N B A R T E N D E R O u U A
I T R E T A I L E R R M N G V
R O E B I K E R Y E O M A N I
R M E R S R E R E T S A L P G
A O N I T R A N R E T N I E A
F L I G H T A T T E N D A N T
L O G A O o H T A P O E T S O
O G N N B N E C S P O R T E R
R I E D O R H G E E S R U N E
I S N E O E S T Y L I S T I G
S T r J R A C E D R I V E R A
T C A R E T A K E R A E O A N
L M R E F L O G R U E T A M A
C O P T S I G R U L L A T E M
```

Secret answer: SURGEON GENERAL

#2, Shopping for Values

```
P R U D E N C E C N E I T A P
S P R O N O H U M I L I T Y x
S T O L E R A N C E I E L E P
E Y A C C O R D A N C E F C U
N T M T I R I P S N M O H N R
D I L P I E T Y A P R T S A I
N S O A A R Y R A G I S N R T
I O V T U T E T I A E H R A Y
K R E T I P H V F N H O P E E
C E H M M Y E Y R E V A R B G
A N A E C N o I R O L A V R A
N E T R E H A R M O N Y P O R
D G E S I F Y T I L E D I F U
O M S S E N T S U J P I T Y O
R I G H T E O U S N E S S c C
```

Secret answer: PHILANTHROPIC

#3, Fowl Play

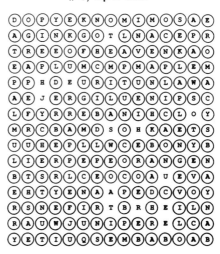

Secret answer: MOURNING DOVE

#4, Up a Tree

Secret answer: THE JOSHUA TREE

#5, Globe Trotting

A C I R F A N I T N E G R A W
U C H R c z D N A L N I F A N
S N H I A I R E G I N G L D I
T E I I N N E R S O H E R N A
R W D T L A E W I A S R O A T
I G N c E E E N N N H M D L I
A U A o C D U I O N B A A E R
I I L E E T S V A O S N V C B
L N O N E T A T L O A Y L I T
A E P I A S S I A s L L A K A
R A V N C I V L o T G v S O E
T O A O K I T A L Y E K L R R
S I T A A K N A L I R S E E G
U I P D N A L E R I I I L A M
A L E U Z E N E V A A A B U C

Secret answer: CZECHOSLOVAKIA

#6, Catch of the Day

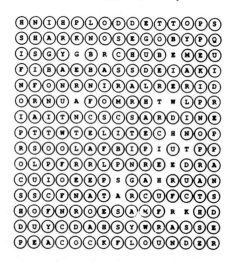

Secret answer: GREAT WHITE SHARK

T H A L L I U M U I N A T I T
A L E K C I N R U F L U S N E
N N E G Y X O O S I L U I M O
T M M M D C C V R E R T R U R
A P U U A N I T R O G E N I I
L L I I E I L A H M B M M V U
U U S C L Z I P U U N U N E M
M T E L D E S I G I I I O L U
U O N A O O H M X N R D G E I
N N G C H T U E A O O O R D C
I I A P E I N R L C N S A N I
T U M M D O U C A R B O N E R
A M O A N A L U M I N U M M E
L R R N O D A R D Z N O E N M
P M U I R T T Y N O M I T N A

Secret answer: SILVER AND GOLD

TRIPLE PLAY

#1

1. handy, gear, hydrangea; 2. paunch, reel, leprechaun; 3. game, strait, magistrate; 4. tuba, slime, sublimate; 5. drain, cone, ordinance; 6. bug, greed, begrudge; 7. stage, moron, gastronome; 8. touch, scene, escutcheon; 9. green, pier, peregrine; 10. dune, oar, rondeau

#2

1. tar, zealot, lazaretto; 2. moors, wire, worrisome; 3. dram, ton, mordant; 4. goat, germ, mortgage; 5. cheat, sum, mustache; 6. stone, limp, simpleton; 7. ear, duct, traduce; 8. bout, marine, tambourine; 9. fate, focus, suffocate; 10. seem, grub, submerge

79

#3

1. spoke, nice, kinescope; 2. keen, rose, kerosene; 3. sum, ulna, alumnus; 4. moth, nap, phantom; 5. seal, top, apostle; 6. radio, mall, armadillo; 7. cater, deep, deprecate; 8. morale, cogent, conglomerate; 9. abate, role, elaborate; 10. grain, milk, grimalkin

#4

1. strain, ace, ascertain; 2. table, gale, bagatelle; 3. gender, vice, divergence; 4. brain, can, cinnabar; 5. rate, rum, erratum; 6. goal, nod, gondola; 7. deign, tear, denigrate; 8. chain, roam, harmonica; 9. nest, gear, estrange; 10. apex, hod, hexapod

#5

1. mud, near, duramen; 2. peat, rote, operetta; 3. tine, coin, nicotine; 4. aegis, peon, espionage; 5. starch, roe, orchestra; 6. navel, red, lavender; 7. love, lament, malevolent; 8. vain, ran, nirvana; 9. pail, moon, palomino; 10. train, club, lubricant

#6

1. curt, none, nocturne; 2. teem, odor, odometer; 3. louse, bun, nebulous; 4. bail, jute, jubilate; 5. rap, tape, parapet; 6. gait, lure, ligature; 7. quill, dear, quadrille; 8. manor, pew, manpower; 9. dew, rage, ragweed; 10. grouse, rat, surrogate

#7

1. crone, hunt, truncheon; 2. tear, door, toreador; 3. magic, leu, mucilage; 4. coat, need, anecdote; 5. reap, teak, parakeet; 6. miser, rube, reimburse; 7. cream, soy, sycamore; 8. queen, chit, technique; 9. phase, more, semaphore; 10. bode, naif, bonafide

#8

1. wrest, acres, watercress; 2. drain, man, mandarin; 3. tea, cream, macerate; 4. gate, lute, tutelage; 5. bout, rust, outburst; 6. ploy, nap, panoply; 7. merit, peer, perimeter; 8. dial, roar, railroad; 9. pine, smart, spearmint; 10. gibe, crab, cribbage

REEL CHALLENGE

#1

1. A Hard Day's Night, Night and Day, Day of the Locust; 2. Sons and Lovers, Lovers and Other Strangers, Strangers on a Train; 3. The Women, Women in Love, Love in the Afternoon; 4. Red River, River of No Return, Return of the Jedi; 5. Bachelor Father, Father of the Bride, Bride of Frankenstein; 6. The Falcon Strikes Back, Back to the Future, Future Cop; 7. Love Me Tender, Tender Is the Night, Night of the Generals; 8. A Patch of Blue, Blue Thunder, Thunder Road; 9. Gross Anatomy, Anatomy of a Murder, Murder by Death; 10. Pretty Woman, Woman Times Seven, Seven Days in May; 11. Mr. North, North by Northwest, Northwest Passage; 12. The L-Shaped Room, Room at the Top, Top Gun; 13. It Happened One Night, Night of the Living Dead, Dead Poet's Society; 14. Around the World in 80 Days, Days of Heaven, Heaven Can Wait; 15. My Fair Lady, Lady in the Dark, Dark Victory

#2

1. Sea of Love, Love and Death, Death on the Nile; 2. Born Yesterday, Yesterday, Today and Tomorrow, Tomorrow Never Comes; 3. Two for the Road, Road to Rio, Rio Bravo; 4. Twelve O'Clock High, High Road to China, China Sky; 5. Round Midnight, Midnight Crossing, Crossing Delancey; 6. Wait Until Dark, Dark Places, Places in the Heart; 7. Reflections in a Golden Eye, Eye of the Tiger, Tiger Bay; 8. Midnight Run, Run Silent, Run Deep, Deep in My Heart; 9. Hester Street, Street People, People Will Talk; 10. The Asphalt Jungle, Jungle Woman, Woman of the Year; 11. The Lion in Winter, Winter Light, Light in the Piazza; 12. So Big, Big Trouble, Trouble in Mind; 13. In Cold Blood, Blood Beach, Beach Blanket Bingo; 14. Thirty Seconds Over Tokyo, Tokyo Joe, Joe Versus the Volcano; 15. The Living Desert, Desert Hearts, Hearts of the West

#3

1. True Confessions, Confessions of a Married Man, Man of a Thousand Faces; 2. The High and the Mighty, Mighty Joe Young, Young Guns; 3. The Heartbreak Kid, Kid Blue, Blue Velvet; 4. The Art of Love, Love with the Proper Stranger, Stranger on Horseback; 5. Some Came Running, Running Scared, Scared Stiff; 6. Animal House, House of Frankenstein, Frankenstein Meets the Wolf Man; 7. For Your Eyes Only, Only Two Can Play, Play Misty for Me; 8. No Way Out, Out of Africa, Africa Screams; 9. Raising Arizona, Arizona Raiders, Raiders of the Seven Seas; 10. The Great Escape, Escape from East Berlin, Berlin Correspondent; 11. An American in Paris, Paris, Texas, Texas Across the River; 12. Black Sunday, Sunday, Bloody Sunday, Sunday in New York; 13. Bright Victory, Victory at Sea, Sea Devils; 14. Scream, Pretty Peggy, Peggy Sue Got Married, Married to the Mob; 15. I Love You, Goodbye, Goodbye, My Fancy, Fancy Pants

#4

1. Storm Warning, Warning Sign, Sign of the Ram; 2. The Wicked Lady, Lady Sings the Blues, Blues for Lovers; 3. A Blueprint for Murder, Murder, My Sweet, Sweet November; 4. Dinner at Eight, Eight Men Out, Out of the Past; 5. Girl Happy, Happy Go Lucky, Lucky Lady; 6. Kiss Me Deadly, Deadly Strangers, Strangers When We Meet; 7. Imitation of Life, Life with Father, Father Goose; 8. The Last Sunset, Sunset Boulevard, Boulevard Nights; 9. A Little Bit of Heaven, Heaven with a Gun, Gun for a Coward; 10. The Killers, Killers Carnival, Carnival of Souls; 11. Carry On, Doctor, Doctor in the House, House Calls; 12. Don't Bother to Knock, Knock on Any Door, Door-to-Door Maniac; 13. The Dead, Dead End, End of the Line; 14. Little Boy Lost, Lost in America, America, America; 15. The Gods Must Be Crazy, Crazy Moon, Moon of the Wolf

#5

1. Betsy's Wedding, Wedding in White, White Heat; 2. Somewhere I'll Find You, You Can't Hurry Love, Love Letters; 3. Middle Age Crazy, Crazy House, House of Cards; 4. Joshua Then and Now, Now and Forever, Forever and a Day; 5. Half Moon Street, Street Music, Music Is Magic; 6. Murphy's Romance, Romance in the Dark, Dark Eyes; 7. Somewhere in Time, Time After Time, Time Bandits; 8. The President's Lady, Lady and the Tramp, Tramp, Tramp, Tramp; 9. Lady Be Good, Good Guys Wear Black, Black Belt Jones; 10. With a Song in My Heart, Heart of Glass, Glass Houses; 11. Dying Young, Young Fury, Fury at Gunfight Pass; 12. Too Scared to Scream, Scream of Fear, Fear No Evil; 13. Fighting Mad, Mad Max, Max Dugan Returns; 14. Lovin' Molly, Molly and Lawless John, John Goldfarb, Please Come Home; 15. Modern Romance, Romance in the Dark, Dark of the Sun

#6

1. I Could Go On Singing, Singing Guns, Guns for San Sebastian; 2. Tobacco Road, Road to Singapore, Singapore Woman; 3. Dark Star, Star in the Dust, Dust Be My Destiny; 4. Postcards from the Edge, Edge of the City, City Limits; 5. Sentimental Journey, Journey into Light, Light of Day; 6. A Lovely Way to Die, Die Hard, Hard, Fast and Beautiful; 7. The Incredible Lightness of Being, Being There, There Was a Crooked Man; 8. The Devil's Rain, Rain Man, Man with a Million; 9. She's Gotta Have It, It Happened at the World's Fair, Fair Wind to Java; 10. Life Begins at Forty, Forty Pounds of Trouble, Trouble in Mind; 11. The Secret Six, Six Hours to Live, Live and Let Die; 12. Sam's Son, Son of Godzilla, Godzilla, King of the Monsters; 13. Hit the Ice, Ice Station Zebra, Zebra in the Kitchen; 14. The Ox-Bow Incident, Incident at Midnight, Midnight Cowboy; 15. I Am Curious Yellow, Yellow Submarine, Submarine Patrol

#7

1. Magnum Force, Force: Five, Five Easy Pieces; 2. The Macomber Affair, Affair with a Stranger, Stranger in My Arms; 3. Lust for Gold, Gold Raiders, Raiders of the Lost Ark; 4. Something Wild, Wild Is the Wind, Wind Across the Everglades; 5. The Last American Hero, Hero and the Terror, Terror Train; 6. Troop Beverly Hills, Hills of Home, Home of the Brave; 7. Duet for Four, Four Hours to Kill, Kill or Be Killed; 8. Foul Play, Play Dirty, Dirty Dingus Magee; 9. A Touch of Class, Class Action, Action Jackson; 10. Earth Girls Are Easy, Easy to Love, Love at First Bite; 11. The Devil's Eight, Eight O'Clock Walk, Walk on the Wild Side; 12. Dirty Little Billy, Billy the Kid, Kid Galahad; 13. Four Rode Out, Out of this World, World Without End; 14. Hearts of the West, West Point Story, Story of a Woman; 15. And Then There Were None, None But the Lonely Heart, Heart Like a Wheel

HALF & HALF

#1

1. Accost, 2. Aspect, 3. Attend, 4. Beggar, 5. Blanch, 6. Dinner, 7. Donate, 8. Enlist, 9. Exhale, 10. Expose, 11. Fescue, 12. Florid, 13. Fought, 14. Gospel, 15. Hazard, 16. Hijack, 17. Hominy, 18. Manual, 19. Orchid, 20. Pantry, 21. Pickle, 22. Poetic, 23. Quarry, 24. Remedy, 25. Shiver, 26. Sister, 27. Speech, 28. Temple, 29. Throne, 30. Torque, 31. Urchin, 32. Verbal

#2

1. Abjure, 2. Abrupt, 3. Animal, 4. Bikini, 5. Canard, 6. County, 7. Domino, 8. Duenna, 9. Dulcet, 10. Ersatz, 11. Father, 12. Feeble, 13. Geyser, 14. Ghetto, 15. Linage, 16. Martyr, 17. Number, 18. Opiate, 19. Permit, 20. Pretty, 21. Raisin, 22. Scream, 23. Tedium, 24. Thesis, 25. Thrill, 26. Tonsil, 27. Unison, 28. Vandal, 29. Vicuna, 30. Vortex, 31. Warren, 32. Whimsy

#3

1. Animus, 2. Anthem, 3. Batten, 4. Behest, 5. Bishop, 6. Brawny, 7. Browse, 8. Degree, 9. Diaper, 10. Effigy, 11. Falcon, 12. Gamble, 13. Intone, 14. Island, 15. Kismet, 16. Lawyer, 17. Madras, 18. Mirror, 19. Muscle, 20. Mutual, 21. Oxford, 22. Penult, 23. People, 24. Pledge, 25. Prefix, 26. Recipe, 27. Resort, 28. Ruffle, 29. Scotch, 30. Scroll, 31. Senary, 32. Travel

#4

1. Bereft, 2. Bridal, 3. Burden, 4. Clamor, 5. Crunch, 6. Finger,
7. Gobbet, 8. Junket, 9. Morgue, 10. Mutton, 11. Mystic, 12. Notary,
13. Nougat, 14. Ocelot, 15. Paddle, 16. Pewter, 17. Rabbit,
18. Reason, 19. Recede, 20. Rustle, 21. Savory, 22. Talent,
23. Tender, 24. Treaty, 25. Update, 26. Vanity, 27. Velvet,
28. Vermin, 29. Vernal, 30. Volume, 31. Weasel, 32. Whisky

#5

1. Brandy, 2. Circus, 3. Cosmos, 4. Damask, 5. Deputy, 6. Futile,
7. Frugal, 8. Gaiety, 9. Gambol, 10. Heaven, 11. Heifer, 12. Ignite,
13. Jargon, 14. Jovial, 15. Knight, 16. Lappet, 17. Magnum,
18. Monism, 19. Oyster, 20. Parody, 21. Preach, 22. Purple,
23. Reflex, 24. Relent, 25. Revoke, 26. Spavin, 27. Subtle, 28. Suffix,
29. Vellum, 30. Vendue, 31. Yellow, 32. Zealot

#6

1. Balsam, 2. Bamboo, 3. Blight, 4. Braise, 5. Burlap, 6. Button,
7. Cattle, 8. Circle, 9. Clover, 10. Crouch, 11. Engine, 12. Expect,
13. Facile, 14. Foster, 15. Genial, 16. Ibidem, 17. Launch,
18. Limber, 19. Marble, 20. Median, 21. Melody, 22. Piracy,
23. Poodle, 24. Porous, 25. Rubric, 26. Sanity, 27. Slogan,
28. Source, 29. Starch, 30. System, 31. Tabard, 32. Violet

#7

1. Allude, 2. Equine, 3. Fedora, 4. Flimsy, 5. Foible, 6. Fossil,
7. Goblin, 8. Grouch, 9. Harrow, 10. Ignore, 11. Isobar, 12. Length,
13. Lesion, 14. Litmus, 15. Pallet, 16. Picket, 17. Pillar, 18. Planet,
19. Prayer, 20. Quaint, 21. Quiver, 22. Radial, 23. Rotund,
24. Scathe, 25. Scenic, 26. Senior, 27. Simple, 28. Siphon,
29. Tickle, 30. Voyeur, 31. Wyvern, 32. Zodiac

CHAIN LETTERS

#1

Hurricane, Tidal wave, Avalanche

#2

Bernstein, Gershwin, Beethoven

#3

Andromeda, Reticulum, Centaurus

#4

Bertolucci, Mankiewicz, Richardson

#5

Innsbruck, Grenoble, Melbourne

#6

Seminole, Iroquois, Kickapoo

MISSING LINKS

#1

#2

#3

#4

#5

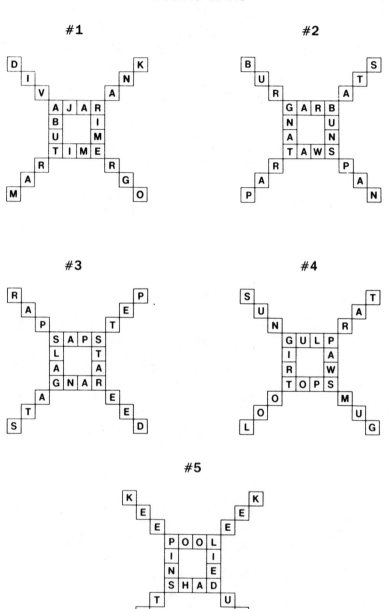

86

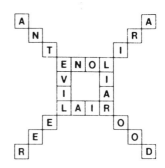

QUOTABLES

#1

1. B, 2. C, 3. A, 4. D, 5. B, 6. D, 7. C, 8. B, 9. C, 10. A

#2

1. A, 2. B, 3. D, 4. A, 5. B, 6. C, 7. B, 8. D, 9. A, 10. C

#3

1. D, 2. B, 3. A, 4. B, 5. C, 6. A, 7. D, 8. B, 9. A, 10. C

#4

1. B, 2. C, 3. D, 4. B, 5. A, 6. B, 7. C, 8. A, 9. D, 10. C

#5

1. A, 2. B, 3. B, 4. A, 5. C, 6. D, 7. C, 8. A, 9. C, 10. B

#6

1. B, 2. A, 3. D, 4. A, 5. C, 6. B, 7. B, 8. D, 9. B, 10. C

#7

1. C, 2. D, 3. A, 4. C, 5. D, 6. B, 7. C, 8. B, 9. A, 10. D

NOW YOU SEE IT

#1, Room for Improvement

"I'm tired of the rattan furniture in this room, Oscar—let's try a new look," Rose said. "Perhaps a quaint country motif or a period look with fetching old accent pieces. Do you agree?" "No," Oscar replied. "I like what we've got."

"Well, I'm extremely impressed by your open mind." Rose answered, her brow nastily arching. "I trust this means we can't even discuss it?"

"Why should we," he shrugged. "You always win every so-called discussion we have, anyway. And neither your intimidation nor anger is going to change my mind. Get my message?"

Rose resorted to her oldest trick: flattery. "I should be nicer, I see that now. But I hate all these big decisions. And you do have excellent taste."

"Well-I-I," Oscar capitulated. "Maybe I did overreact. Just do whatever you like. Your choice of decor always pleases me."

"Why, Oscar, you're the most romantic fool I've ever known," Rose gushed, and immediately called her decorator.

red, tan, scarlet, rose, aqua, gold, green, lime, brown, rust, wine, orange, sage, cerise, teal, dove, coral, olive

#2, Survival of the Fittest

It was his first agonizing day on the job, and the new entertainment director at the retirement center ate little during lunch.

"I'm afraid the kayak excursion will be entirely too strenuous for these senior citizens," he fretted to himself, pushing his plate aside while fishing for the aspirin tin in his pocket. "And what if they're not terribly fond of scuba diving or water volleyball, either?"

He swallowed hard, scowling as he realized there wasn't one land activity in which he could confidently supervise them unless, he thought suddenly, they liked bowling. Of course! The idea of bowling was perfectly brilliant—a great way to stay in shape and share a group activity, too!

But when the young director proposed they have a go at it, the seniors groused loudly. "Bowling is out of the question, you overbearing nuisance," declared one. "Training for the Olympic Decathlon demands quite enough of our time, thank you!"

stag, hen, ewe, rat, ratel, yak, cur, bee, fish, asp, otter, cub, swallow, cow, eland, emu, owl, ling, wasp, ant, ape, hare, goat, grouse, bear, gnu, cat

#3, Looking Out for Number One

Eva seemed quieter than usual, Arthur thought. She wasn't very animated, and even that chic hairdo she'd had Ivan give her yesterday was now limp and drab.

When asked how she felt, Eva appeared to welcome the attention. "My head aches terribly," she fretted, "and I feel so faint. Forgive me for moping around like this."

"Let's hop in the car, pet, and take you to see Dr. Apelgren," Arthur said. "He can prescribe some drugs to help you. But we should be doing something now—not later."

"Relax, dear," said Eva. "There's no need to get the least overwrought. But," she added, giving him a mock rap on his chin, "any ailing lass would be bowled over by such attentiveness."

Arthur was too embarrassed to tell her that he'd actually been thinking, "If I don't keep Eva's health stable, then who'll take care of me?" So he simply replied, with hardly a trace of irony in his voice, "Any husband worth his salt would do the same, love!"

vase, art, tv, mat, chair, divan, pan, towel, chest, sofa, mop, pin, carpet, key, drape, crib, rug, bed, stove, china, glass, bowl, bar, table, iron, salt

#4, The Art of the Short Story

Entering through a gate in back, Opal Emery caught her two grandchildren totally by surprise. As they ran to her, she headed for the porch swing, saying, "Okay—last one on my lap is a rotten egg!"

"Sticks and stones may break my bones, but names can never hurt me," they chimed in unison, as each pounced on an empty knee.

"Will you tell us a story?" asked Ruby, the older child.

"Not unless Hale stops squirming," Opal replied, with a jaded glance at her grandson. He smiled shyly and snuggled closer, savoring the smell of the talcum his grandmother always wore. Then he sneezed, his nose tickled by an unseen piece of lint in the air.

"Bless you," Opal said, then she began. "Since it's late, I'll tell you a tale my first teacher told me—a very short ghost story, as I recall," she said slyly, "about a ghost who was simply too short to be the subject of a tall tale." And on that note, she arose and left.

"That Gran—I tell you, she's a card," said Ruby, watching her depart.

"One who should be dealt with!" Hale grinned, repeating one of Opal's favorite puns. Laughing, they resumed playing.

agate, opal, emery, lapis, sandstone, ruby, shale, jade, talc, flint, slate, chert, granite

#5, Ducking the Issue

Dickie Chatham took umbrage at his school's mascot: a duck! Seething, he wondered which dumb louses had suggested such a name, and how the situation could best be addressed.

He'd go right to the top, Dickie decided. He'd just find the courage and stamina to talk to the principal and make short shrift of the matter. The outcome was inescapable—a new mascot would be chosen by the student body.

Sashaying into the principal's office, he explained his purpose. "Oh, pshaw," lisped the secretary, Jean Smithers, through her braces. "He's never in during the mornings, but he'll be returning this afternoon."

Through the window behind her, Dickie was watching as the principal's car flashed by. Following his gaze, she said, "He's early! No sweat, sir—I'll get you in right away."

After the meeting, Dickie felt defeated. The principal, haughtier than ever, had refused to give the idea even minimum consideration. Pursing his lips and with no vestige of warmth, he recited the school's motto instead: "If it's your luck to be a duck, then never, ever run amuck; just stay the course and mark my word—you'll always be the early bird!"

Dickie never forgot. After graduation he entered medical school, and became a very wealthy quack.

dickie, hat, bra, ascot, ducks, blouse, dress, top, tam, shorts, cap, hose, stud, sash, shawl, jeans, braces, ring, beret, watch, scarf, sweats, tie, mini, slip, vest, bead

#6, Ordering à la Carte

"It appears that my friend, Allen Tilton, has set a date for his one-man art show," Cornelia Green said, smiling at her handsome male secretary, "and nothing will appease him if I don't attend. So be a nice fellow and cancel my trip to San Antonio next week, Alex."

"That won't take me long," he replied. "Anything else?"

"Yes. You escort me to the show, and in return, I promote you to administrative assistant."

"You're very generous," Alex said, and as he studied her sleek demeanor, anger washed over him. "But why would you promote me?"

"Because I don't socialize with mere secretaries!"

"I never figured you for such a snob," Alex shot back. "Now that I know what a witch I've been working for, you can have your job back!"

"It may amuse you to know that I'd hoped for this reaction," Cornelia smiled. "Now we can see each other without my having to worry about dating an employee!"

"Not in this lifetime," Alex said, "and not in Tilton's, either. Every time I see his so-called art, I choke!"

A week later, Cornelia forgot all about Alex when the receptionist buzzed her on the intercom to say, "Your new secretary, Brad, is here . . . will that be two for lunch?"

pear, lentil, date, corn, greens, pea, bean, onion, kale, melon, turnip, leek, orange, fig, chive, yam, artichoke, radish

#7, First Things First

Jack's mom, Dolly Glover, was always on the ball where her son was concerned. She cared deeply about his welfare and giving him a proper education, constantly drumming into his head, "Carouse less and study more, don't let important things slide, plan every move before you jump, and always remember—books are your friends!"

Jack found it hard to mask his impatience with her prattle and dogma. They struck him as unnecessary, and he wished she'd stop lecturing him.

He was more at home with a hoop and, given a ball, could slam-dunk it every time. So sure was he of a pro career, in fact, that Jack didn't even intend or aspire to graduate.

When Dolly found out, the lines of battle were drawn. She grounded Jack until he finished college five years later and signed with the team of his choice.

A multimillionaire when he retired, Jack attributed his success to his mother. "She's the best friend and most worthy opponent I've ever had," he said, "and she never even got called for goal tending!"

jacks, doll, glove, ball, car, rope, cat, drum, carousel, slide, plane, panda, books, mask, rattle, dog, truck, top, hoop, kite, Nintendo, bat, slate, tire

SPELLBINDERS

#1

"E-T-E-S-R"

T	E	R	S	E
S	T	E	E	R
E	S	T	E	R
T	R	E	E	S
R	E	S	E	T

"R-I-T-P-S-E"

S	T	R	I	P	E
P	R	I	E	S	T
E	S	P	R	I	T
S	P	R	I	T	E
R	I	P	E	S	T

#2

"L-S-E-T-A"

S	L	A	T	E
T	A	L	E	S
S	T	A	L	E
S	T	E	A	L
L	E	A	S	T

"S-R-T-A-C-E"

T	R	A	C	E	S
C	A	R	E	T	S
C	R	A	T	E	S
R	E	A	C	T	S
C	A	S	T	E	R

#3

"A-R-S-P-E"

S	P	A	R	E
R	E	A	P	S
P	A	R	E	S
S	P	E	A	R
P	E	A	R	S

"W-E-R-R-A-D"

R	E	W	A	R	D
D	R	A	W	E	R
W	A	R	R	E	D
R	E	D	R	A	W
W	A	R	D	E	R

92

"E-B-T-A-S"

B	A	S	T	E
A	B	E	T	S
B	E	A	T	S
B	E	A	S	T
B	A	T	E	S

"P-T-S-A-E-L"

S	T	A	P	L	E
P	L	A	T	E	S
P	A	S	T	E	L
P	L	E	A	T	S
P	E	T	A	L	S

"P-S-L-A-E"

L	A	P	S	E
P	L	E	A	S
L	E	A	P	S
P	A	L	E	S
S	E	P	A	L

"V-L-E-S-R-A"

R	A	V	E	L	S
S	L	A	V	E	R
L	A	V	E	R	S
S	A	L	V	E	R
S	E	R	V	A	L

"N-T-O-S-E"

S	T	O	N	E
T	O	N	E	S
O	N	S	E	T
N	O	T	E	S
S	T	E	N	O

"T-C-A-R-E-N"

R	E	C	A	N	T
C	A	N	T	E	R
T	R	A	N	C	E
C	E	N	T	R	A
N	E	C	T	A	R

"I-E-S-N-R"

S	I	R	E	N
R	I	S	E	N
R	E	S	I	N
R	E	I	N	S
R	I	N	S	E

"I-M-T-E-S-R"

M	I	S	T	E	R
R	E	M	I	T	S
M	E	R	I	T	S
M	I	T	E	R	S
T	I	M	E	R	S

94

MYSTERY MAZE

#1

Colon, Dinar, Krone, Lira, Peso, Pound, Rand, Riel, Rupee, Sucre, Yen, Yuan

#2

Aries, Leo, Libra, Pisces, Scorpio, Taurus, Virgo

#3

Cello, Clarinet, Flute, Harp, Oboe, Trumpet, Tuba

#4

Basil, Capers, Dill, Marjoram, Mint, Oregano, Sage

#5

Cod, Crab, Haddock, Halibut, Shad, Shrimp, Trout, Tuna, Turbot

#6

Anise, Cloves, Cumin, Paprika, Pepper, Vanilla

#7

Diamond, Emerald, Garnet, Opal, Ruby, Topaz

INDEX

Pages shown in boldface contain the answers.